AF173623

Words

Words are all around us – but taking them in and learning to use them appropriately takes time. As parents, we generally buy a thesaurus, dictionaries and other resources to make word learning accessible to our children. Unfortunately, vocabulary cannot be improved merely by encountering new words. They need to be retained in the memory and should be actively used. We need to raise word consciousness in children by playing with words through games, songs and art. Learning new words can be tricky if we don't know the ways of understanding and retaining them. We all know that the more a memory is used, the more it endures. Repeated exposure is one of the best ways to master new vocabulary. Children must engage with a word several times in different contexts before it is learned. Researchers suggest that children need to encounter a new word 4 to 12 times in order to retain it in their vocabulary.

Encourage children to keep a word jar or word journal, and add new words to it regularly. Ask them to review the words from time to time. Make word learning a game. The aim of the book is to make the learning process joyous and fascinating for children, and provide techniques that will improve quick word learning.

Seven techniques for becoming a word master!

1. Word categorisation. Words are classified into parts of speech and are named according to their function in a sentence. It is imperative to work smart while learning new words. An effective way of doing so is to learn the word with its part of speech and practice changing the word into a different part of speech. Through this technique, children will be able to understand the meaning and the function of words in a sentence. This will help them to learn the use of the new word.

2. Word fragmentation. Words can be broken down into fragments by identifying a root word, prefix or suffix. Many words contain a root word, and if children know the meaning of the root word, it's easier for them to understand the new word. For example, by knowing that the meaning of the root word mal is bad, it's easier for children to comprehend the meaning of words containing that root, such as malevolent and malfunction. Knowledge of prefixes and suffixes along with their meaning can help children to derive the meaning of the words to which they are attached.

3. Word association. Words relate to other words. Encouraging children to draw connections between an unfamiliar word and one they know bolsters their understanding of both words; it could be by knowing synonyms, antonyms or a root word. Knowing

more about a word broadens their understanding and enables them to use it more confidently. Learning a word with multiple meanings is also a great way to enhance their vocabulary list.

4. Wordoodle. Connecting a word to a vivid visual image is another way to learn new words easily, as movements and images facilitate vocabulary learning. A strong image sticks in the mind for a long time. It's easy to create a picture in our mind when we see a phrase. The more vivid the image, the better we learn. Our brain loves context and thus links a given word with different sensory perceptions. *For example:* to link the word *adept* to its meaning, explain the meaning in your own words and say a phrase using the word. The phrase, an adept piano player, can assist children to visualise a vivid image of someone playing the piano seamlessly. Asking children to doodle a symbol or a picture that represents some aspect of the meaning helps them in retaining the word in their long-term memory.

5. Acting out the word. Using multiple senses allows more cognitive connections. By acting out words through facial expression or action, children engage multiple senses and hence create a multisensory experience. This accelerates and expands the way the information can be triggered and retrieved from their cognitive learning centre, which helps them remember and retain information more effectively. This technique easily engages children to learn enthusiastically.

6. Guessing the meaning. Reading augments vocabulary and enhances the ability to use the words effectively. Using context clues to understand a new word is a great way to enhance vocabulary. It is sometimes possible to figure out the meaning of a word by the way it is used in a sentence. Children should be encouraged to use this technique while reading, and then check the dictionary to find the actual meaning of words. This technique encourages self-checking, which further helps memory retention. This will lead to a unique journey of learning the word using the child's own perception and ability.

7. Replacing overused words. Making a list of overused words and replacing them with the more sophisticated ones helps children widen their vocabulary and improves their writing skills. Children consciously engage with new words to replace frequently used ones and will therefore learn the new words effortlessly.

 Fab**V**OCAB

Let's introduce you to some vocabulary buddies who will appear throughout this book to make word learning easy.

Star symbol represents new words that you have not encountered before and would like to add to your word list. Your aim should be to collect as many star words as you can and apply the techniques given in this booklet to learn them. It will be awesome if you include these star words in your writing and daily conversation.

'Ann' likes to collect antonyms. Ann likes to challenge the norm and always has an opposite view on everything.

'Sym' symbol represents Synonyms. Sym likes to collect synonyms. Sym is vibrant, active and loves to find similar-meaning words.

Wordoodle symbol. When this symbol appears, it means that you should try to doodle the word that is listed with it. Sometimes it's easier to learn the meaning of a word by associating it with a special icon or drawing a doodle that represents some aspect of its meaning. You can Wordoodle either the word itself, its synonym or its antonym. It sometimes becomes easier to break up a word and then try to doodle a section or the whole word to learn the new word. Happy doodling!

Word Classification

Sentences are made up of words and each word in a sentence belongs to a particular class, depending on how it is used. These classes are called parts of speech. Thus, words are classified into parts of speech and are named according to their function in a sentence. It is imperative to work smart while learning new words.

An effective way of doing so is to learn the word with its part of speech. Understanding the different parts of speech is important in understanding how words can and should be joined together to make sentences that are both grammatically correct and readable. Through this technique, you are not only able to understand the meaning, but also the function of the word in a sentence.

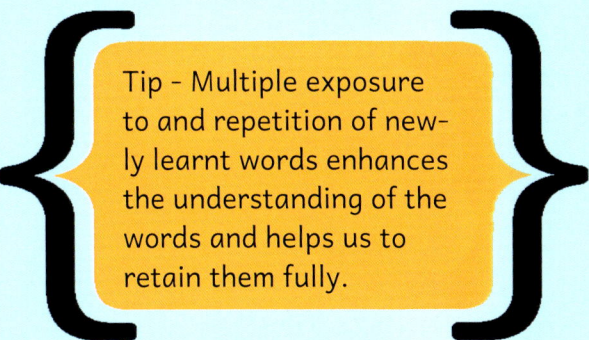

{ Tip – Multiple exposure to and repetition of newly learnt words enhances the understanding of the words and helps us to retain them fully. }

Remember

Repetition and multiple exposures to vocabulary words are important. Children should be provided with opportunities to encounter words repeatedly and in a variety of contexts. Did you know that research indicates that a child needs 12 instructional encounters to learn and fully know a word? These exposures should be in variety of contexts, ranging from listening to the word in a conversation, finding it in a book, from the media and many other sources, and using in their writing. Also, seeing the same word in the context of different parts of speech enhances multiple exposure and provides a complete understanding of the word.

Glee – noun; gleeful – adjective; gleefully – adverb

Annoy – verb; annoyance – noun; annoying – adjective

Benevolence – noun; benevolent – adjective; benevolently – adverb

Persuade – verb; persuasion – noun; persuasive – adjective

 **Fab V OCAB**

Hi, I am Sym. I love words and would like to share my knowledge of words with you.

Hey! I am Ann. Do you know that words are categorised according to their function in a sentence? The parts of speech explain how a word is used. The main parts of speech are: nouns, pronouns, adjectives, verbs, adverbs, prepositions, interjections and conjunctions.

 **WORDS**

ADJECTIVES

Adjective: an adjective gives more information about a noun. Adjectives help us describe or pick out which particular thing among many is being referred to. Adjectives are sometimes called 'describing words'.
Examples – easy, hard, thrilling, clever.

ADVERBS

Adverb: an adverb gives information about the way that an action is carried out or when and where it takes place.
Examples- slowly, quickly, hesitantly, reluctantly.

 **VERBS**

Verb: a verb tells us about an action or a state of being.
Examples – run, fall, eat, wonder.

NOUNS

Noun: a word that labels a thing or an idea. Nouns are sometimes called 'naming words'.
Examples – Lizzie, London.

PRONOUNS

Pronoun: a word that is used instead of a noun or a noun phrase.
Examples – he, she, they, we, it, them, us.

PREPOSITIONS

Preposition: a preposition is one of a small group of words that can be used with nouns and verbs. Prepositions give information about position or movement.
Examples- in, on, under, above, beneath, over, at.

INTERJECTIONS

Interjections are words that express excitement or emotions.
Examples -wow! oh no, phew

CONJUNCTIONS

Conjunction: a conjunction joins two or more nouns or clauses to each other. Conjunctions are sometimes called 'joining words'.
Examples- and, but, because, so therefore, although, yet.

Fab**V**OCAB

Categorising Words

Words are classified into parts of speech and are named according to their function in a sentence. It is imperative to work smart while learning new words. An effective way of doing so is to learn words as parts of speech and practise changing words into a different part of speech. You will be able to understand the meaning and function of the word in a sentence.

WEEK 1

Example: Slowly, Ryan ambled back to the new car.
Can you list different parts of speech in the sentence given above?
Nouns:
Verb:
Adjective:
Adverb:

▶ **Activity 1**

Change nouns into verb.

	Noun	Verb
1.	procrastination	
2.	beautician	
3.	completion	
4.	enhancement	
5.	embarkation	
6.	persuasion	

▶ **Activity 2**

Change adjectives into adverb.

	Adjective	Adverb
1.	fabulous	
2.	diligent	
3.	benevolent	
4.	astute	
5.	avid	
6.	meek	

FabVOCAB

You have learnt so far

(Parts of speech)

▶ **Activity 3**

Choose the words given in the box and write each word in the column that it belongs to.

happiness	breezy		yet	adoringly	without

happiness   breezy   yet   adoringly   without
        despite   copious   whoever
since   annually   none
    they   spectacular   thanks   cheers   several
regarding   whenever   should   after
        before   tomorrow
            everybody
cantankerous   hello   seem   milk
        myself   ocean
audience   phew   congratulations
            country   coarse
savagely   been   under   ouch   as long as
    although   clean
across   sprint
    statue of liberty   extremely
            shaggy   gaze

nouns					
pronouns					
adjectives					
verbs					
adverbs					
preposi-tions					
conjunc-tions					
interjec-tions					

Word Fragmentation

Words can be broken down into fragments by identifying a root word, prefix or suffix. Many words contain a root word, and if children know the meaning of the root word, it's easier for them to understand the new word: e.g. by knowing the meaning of the root word mal, which means 'bad' or 'evil', it is easier for children to comprehend the meaning of the words containing that root and recall that mal means 'bad' through words such as malfunction, which means the bad working of a part or system, or malice, which means an evil intention towards another.

The knowledge that prefixes can alter the meaning of words can further help children to extend their vocabulary. Researchers agree that the more a learner engages with a new word, the more likely they are to learn it. By building in opportunities to have fun with words, children get engaged, reinforce their vocabulary and are motivated to learn them.

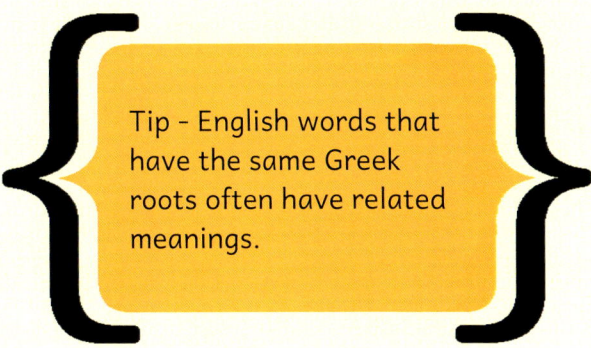

Tip - English words that have the same Greek roots often have related meanings.

Words that starts with 'ph-' are usually of Greek origin, for example: philosophy, physical, photo, phrase, philanthropy.

phobia (fear of), as in arachnophobia – the fear of spiders

micro (small), as in microscopic – so small it's hard to see

chrono (time) - chronic, synchronize, chronicle

jur (law) - jury, justice, justify

 **Fab V OCAB**

Hi, there! Do you know a word can be broken down into parts?

Spot On!

Hmm... ! I guess, I know. Are you talking about root words, prefixes and suffixes?

WEEK 2

This week, you will be learning about ROOT WORDS, PREFIXES AND SUFFIXES.

Remember - Word knowledge can be expanded by knowing the root words.

Many words we use have a root word. When we take the prefix or suffix away from the word, the root word is displayed. Each root word has its own meaning; if you understand the meaning of the root word, it becomes easier to understand the meaning of the word containing the root. You can use the spelling of the root word to help spell the new word too.

Example -

The root word Bene has its origin in the Latin word **"bene"** which means well and is used to convey goodness and wellness.

Let's add the root word 'Bene' to make some new words.
1.   Bene**ficial** -   brings a positive result
2.   Bene**volent** - kind
3.   Bene**fit** - advantage
4.   Bene**factor** - A person who gives money or helps others
5.   Bene**ficiary** - recipient of gifts

▶ **Activity 4**   Find the origin of the root word **VARI** and its meaning. Try to make six new words using the root word VARI.

1. --
2. --
3. --
4. --
5. --

VARI- (meaning) (origin)

You have learnt so far

(Parts of speech) (Root words)

▶ **Activity 5**

Identify the root words in the following words and write the meaning of the root word. Can you derive the meaning of the words containing the same root word?

1.

root word - Bio	meaning - life	origin - Greek
Biology	study of living things.	
Biography	an account of someone's life, written by someone else.	
Biodegradable	capable of being decomposed by bacteria or other living organisms.	

2.

root word -	meaning -	origin -
Paternal		
Patriarch		
Paternity		

3.

root word -	meaning -	origin -
Design		
Signal		
Signature		

4.

root word -	meaning -	origin -
Introspect		
Spectacle		
Spectre		

5.

root word -	meaning -	origin -
Generate		
Progeny		
Genesis		

6.

root word -	meaning -	origin -
Chronological		
Chronical		
Synchronise		

Prefixes and suffixes

A prefix- is a word part placed in front of a word that changes the word's meaning.

	Prefix	Meaning	Example word
1.	in	not	incomplete
2.	im	not	impolite
3.	inter	between	interact
4.	re	again	reappear
5.	ex	out	exhale
6.	mis	bad	misbehave

A suffix – is a word part placed at the end of a word.

	Suffix	Meaning	Example word
1.	less	without	tasteless
2.	able	having the quality of	enjoyable
3.	ly	in the stated way	slowly
4.	er	comparative	smarter
5.	est	superlative	smartest
6.	ful	full of	wonderful

▶ **Activity 6 - Make new words using the prefixes and suffixes given below.**

	word	prefix	new word	meaning
1.	correct	in	incorrect	not correct
2.	approve	dis		
3.	behave	mis		
4.	tell	re		
5.	conventional	un		

	word	suffix	new word	meaning
1.	heart	less		
2.	beauty	ful		
3.	love	able		
4.	affectionate	ly		
5.	smart	est		

You have learnt so far

(Part of speech) (Root words) (Prefixes and suffixes)

Practice task 1 – Week 2

This week your task is to find ten different root words, write down their meaning, and spot words that contain those root words.

Words	Meaning	Origin

Can you make a **word spider** using the root word **con** and derive five new words from it? Don't forget to check the meaning of the words using a dictionary.

root word – con	meaning – jointly, with	origin – Latin

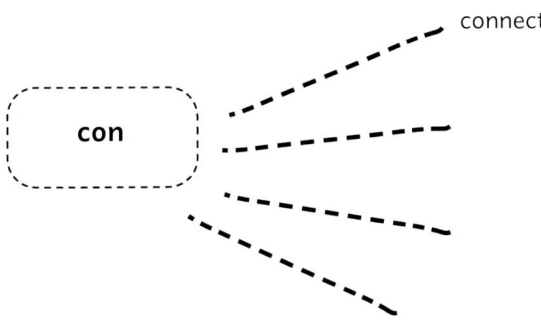

Word Relationships

Words relate to other words, and have multiple meanings too. When you draw connections between an unfamiliar word and a relatable one, it bolsters the understanding of both words. It could be through knowing synonyms, antonyms, homophones, a root word or multiple meaning of the newly learned word. Knowing more about a word will broaden your understanding of it and enable you to use it more confidently. It is vital that you should be able to integrate the new word with existing knowledge.

Do you know that as many as 70% of the most commonly used words have multiple meanings, possessing either fine shades of difference or unrelated meanings? But interestingly, the meanings of 60% of the new words you encounter can be inferred by analysing word parts. Clearly, knowing a word well requires complex understandings.

> Example: word relationship of the word *weak*;
> synonyms– fragile, feeble, frail;
> antonyms – strong, robust, brawny;
> homophone – week

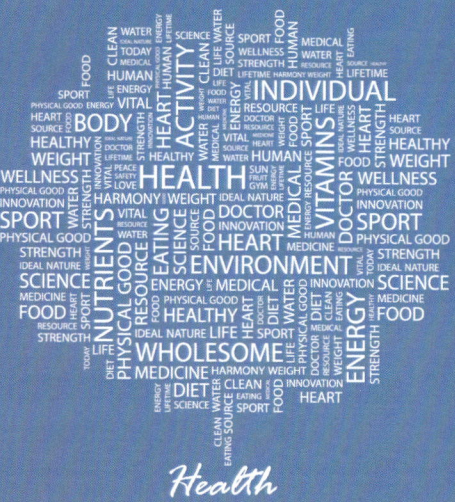

Health

Tip: To retain a new word in your long-term memory, it is essential to review it after regular intervals. The long-term memory stores the things that we never forget. Research shows that when you learn something new from books or lessons, you'll forget more than half of it within days. But if you spend a few minutes reviewing the information at regular intervals such as weekly reviews, your ability to recall it will be vastly improved, because when you review something again and again your brain stores the facts in long-term memory. This technique works magically. Flash cards and word jars can be a handy way to review words again and again. You can make it a daily ritual to learn a new word and review it on weekly basis.

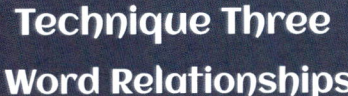

WEEK 3

This week, you will be learning about SYNONYMS and ANTONYMS.

Remember – Every word has multiple meanings.

I am going to Echo valley. Do you want to join me, Sym?

What are we going to do there?

It is a magical place. Shout out a word and you will see the magic. You will hear similar meaning words echoing across one end and opposite meaning words from another end.

Draw connections between what you know about the unfamiliar word. It could be knowing its synonyms or antonyms. **Learning synonyms and antonyms of a word broadens your understanding of the word and enables you to use the word more confidently**. It is also good to note if the word has multiple meanings. Try to learn different meanings of new words.

Echo Valley

▶ Activity 7 | In this activity, you need to find out three synonyms and antonyms of the words given below.

1. Amenable (adjective)

meaning:

If you are **amenable** to something, you are willing to do it or accept it.

receptive

responsive

open

uncooperative

resistant

umamenable

2. Dismal (adjective)

meaning:

Something which is bad in a sad or depressing way.

3. Proficient (adjective)

meaning:

If you are **proficient** in something, you can do it well.

4. Taciturn (adjective)

meaning:

A **taciturn** person does not say very much and can seem unfriendly.

5. Audacious (adjective)

meaning:

Someone who is **audacious** takes risks in order to achieve something.

6. Obstinate (adjective)

meaning:

you describe someone as **obstinate**; you are being critical of them because they are very determined to do what they want, and refuse to change their mind or be persuaded to do something else.

7. Exuberant (adjective)

meaning:

If you are **exuberant**, you are full of energy, excitement, and cheerfulness.

8. Oblivious (adjective)

meaning:

If you are **oblivious** to something or oblivious of it, you are not aware of it.

9. Riveting (adjective)

meaning:

If you describe something as **riveting**, you mean that it is extremely interesting and exciting.

10. Exquisite (adjective)

meaning:

something that is **exquisite** is extremely beautiful or pleasant, especially in a delicate way.

11. Petrified (adjective)

meaning:

if you are **petrified,** you are extremely frightened.

12. Exasperated (adjective)

meaning:

If you describe a person as **exasperated,** you mean that they are frustrated or angry.

13. Apprehensive (adjective)

meaning:

Someone who is **apprehensive** is afraid that something bad may happen.

14. Destitute (adjective)

meaning:

Someone who is **destitute** has no money or possessions.

15. Savage (adjective)

meaning:

Someone or something that is **savage** is extremely cruel.

You have learnt so far

(Part of speech) (Root words) (Prefixes and suffixes) (Synonyms and Antonyms)

Practice task 2 - Week 3

Collect **twenty** ⭐ words this week and research two synonyms and two antonyms of each word. You are free to use a thesaurus to complete this task.

Word	Synonyms	Antonyms

 Fab**V**OCAB

Wordoodle or visualising the word

Do you know that multisensory experiences such as acting out a word and doodling can help you retain new words in your memory? Movements and images facilitate vocabulary learning. It becomes easier for us to learn a new word if we connect the word to a vivid visual image A strong image sticks in the mind for a long time and it's easy to create a picture in our mind when we hear a phrase containing the word. The more vivid the image is the better we learn as brain links a given word with different sensory perceptions.

For example: to link the word *adept* to its meaning, explain the meaning in your own words and say a phrase using the word. The phrase, *an adept piano player*, can assist you to visualise a vivid image of someone playing piano seamlessly. You can even doodle a symbol or a picture that represents some aspect of the meaning which further assists you in retaining the word in your long-term memory. This technique can especially help you learn homophones.

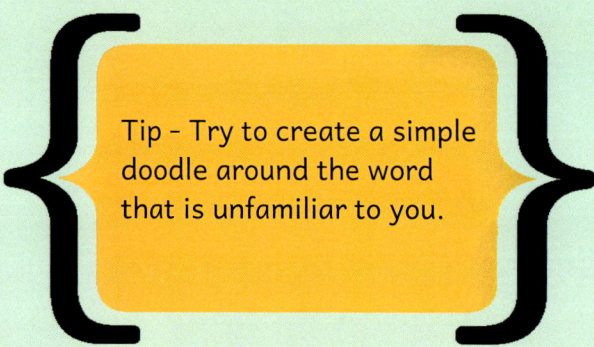

{ Tip - Try to create a simple doodle around the word that is unfamiliar to you. }

An example of wordoodle for the word LONDON can look life.

Connect the word to a vivid visual image. A strong image sticks in the mind for a long time. It's easy to create a picture in our mind when we see a phrase. The more vivid the image is the better we will learn. And remember our brain loves context.

Represent the word with a doodle or a symbol. You may doodle within a single alphabet or around the whole word. The idea is to doodle in such a way that it reflects the meaning of the word.

Humming homophones

Sail boat

Boat for sale

Tranquil Quay

Antique keys

Rose garden

Flowery rows

Wow! Echo valley was wonderful!

Where are we heading to, now? Oh! This signpost is so confusing! The words sound similar but do they have the same meaning?

I know, these are homophones! These are the words that sound similar but have different meaning and are also spelled differently.

I know a technique that makes it easier to learn homophones. It's called Wordoodle.

WEEK 4

This week, you will learn about **HOMOPHONES.**

Remember - It's time to use Wordoodle in this technique.

► **Activity 8** Find the meaning of the homophones given below. Visualise or doodle an image next to the word that relates to its meaning.

sle

isle

(noun) Meaning - **small island, land surrounded by water**	*(noun) Meaning -* **passageway dividing something, passage, corridor**

discreet

discrete

(adjective) Meaning -

(adjective) Meaning -

eminent

imminent

(adjective) Meaning -

(adjective) Meaning -

extant

extent

(adjective) Meaning -

(noun) Meaning -

precede

proceed

(verb) Meaning -

(verb) Meaning -

insight

(noun) Meaning -

incite

(verb) Meaning -

principal

(noun) Meaning -

principle

(noun) Meaning -

peal

(noun) Meaning -

peel

(noun) Meaning -

currant

(noun) Meaning -

current

(adjective) Meaning -

descent

(noun) Meaning -

dissent

(noun) Meaning -

bough

(noun) Meaning -

bow

(noun) Meaning -

waive

(verb) Meaning -

wave

(noun) Meaning -

quire

(noun) Meaning -

choir

(noun) Meaning -

hoard

(noun) Meaning -

horde

(noun) Meaning -

vain

(adjective) Meaning -

vein

(noun) Meaning -

You have learnt so far

Practice task 3 - Week 4

This week your task is to collect five homophones to add to your ⭐ words list. Use Wordoodle to learn their meanings.

Act out the word

You can harness more brain power when you use more than one sensory system at once. Using multiple senses to learn something new creates more cognitive connections and associations with a concept. By acting out the words, you can engage multiple senses and create a vivid experience. By doing so, you will form multiple sets of connections; those various sets of connections are all related to the same learning experience. This means that newly acquired information becomes more easily accessible to you because there are more ways the information can be triggered and retrieved from memory later on, which helps you remember and retain information more effectively. I bet this technique will straightaway engage you, and you will love playing this game to learn new words. This technique is similar to a dumb charades game that you can play at home, in school or on the go. Remember, sometimes it's easier to memorise the meaning by acting out the word. This exercise can be done with a friend or your own. Check the meaning using a dictionary and then act out the word and ask your partner to guess its meaning by looking at your facial expressions and body gestures.

{ Tip - You can use this technique on your own by acting out in front of the mirror. }

Acting out words by actions or facial expressions can help you learn the word easily.

WEEK 5

This week, you will learn about ADVERBS.

Remember - Words can be acted out to enhance understanding.

Sometimes it's easier to memorise the meaning by acting out the word. This exercise can be done with a friend or your own. Once you have guessed the meaning of the word, describe its meaning in your own words.

Check the meaning in the dictionary. Try to collect at least two synonyms of the word.

Hey! Look emoticons!

Super!

Shall we play a game where you will act out an emotion and I will try to guess it?

FabOCAB

Amazing Adverbs

 Activity 9   **Can you act out the adverbs given below?**
In this activity you need to find out the meaning of a word and then try to act it out to cement its understanding.

Write the meaning in your own words.

----

1.   Bashfully

Write the meaning in your own words.

----

2.   Sheepishly

Write the meaning in your own words.

----

3.   Hysterically

Write the meaning in your own words.

----

4.   Woefully

Write the meaning in your own words.

----

5.   Valiantly

Write the meaning in your own words.

----

6.   Obnoxiously

Write the meaning in your own words.

----

7.   **Affectionately**

Write the meaning in your own words.

----

8.   **Strenuously**

Write the meaning in your own words.

----

9.   **Avidly**

Write the meaning in your own words.

----

10.   Briskly

Write the meaning in your own words.

----

11.   Coaxingly

Write the meaning in your own words.

----

12.   Vivaciously

Write the meaning in your own words.

----

13.   Elegantly

Write the meaning in your own words.

----

14.   Outrageously

Write the meaning in your own words.

----

15.   Queasily

Act out the word

You have learnt so far

(Part of speech) (Root words) (Prefixes and suffixes) (Synonyms and Antonyms) (Homophones) (Adverbs)

Practice task 4 - Week Five

This week, use the list of words below, find out their meanings and try to show those meanings through your expression. Make a note of the action that you perform to express each word. You can ask a friend or a family member to help complete this task.

Example- (Petrified) What expressions do you see on someone's face when they are petrified? Can you imitate the expression?

	Word	Describe the action	Actual meaning
1.	Petrified	Trembling hands, feet fixed to one spot	extremely scared
2.	Bewildered		
3.	Jubilant		
4.	Aggressive		
5.	Concerned		
6.	Doleful		
7.	Embarrassed		
8.	Frustrated		
9.	Inquisitive		
10.	Lethargic		
11.	Nervous		
12.	Panicked		
13.	Relaxed		
14.	Spiteful		
15.	Worried		

Guess the meaning

Reading augments vocabulary and enhances the ability to use new words effectively. Using context clues to understand a new word is a great way to enhance vocabulary. It is sometimes easier to figure out the meaning of a word by the way it is used in a sentence. You should use this technique while reading. You can underline or highlight the word you don't understand. After the reading time, you should refer back to the text and try to decipher its meaning, and then use a thesaurus or dictionary to confirm or correct it. This leads to a unique journey of learning a new word, as you first try to work out its meaning using your own perception and ability by analysing the surrounding text. If the answer is wrong, you will retry and analyse it again. In this process, you will cement and comprehend the meaning fully and also learn how newly learnt word can be used in writing. Research shows that when words and easy-to-understand explanations are introduced in context, knowledge of those words increases and word meanings are better learned. Also, when an unfamiliar word is likely to affect comprehension, the most effective time to introduce its meaning may be at the moment it is met in the text.

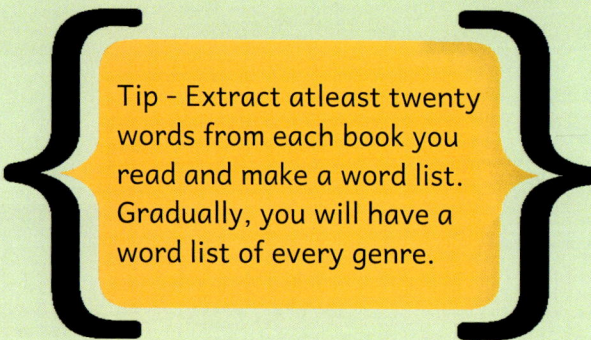

Tip - Extract atleast twenty words from each book you read and make a word list. Gradually, you will have a word list of every genre.

Try deciphering the meaning of the word **'feretted'** *in the example sentence below.*
Mrs. Rachel was sitting at her window, keeping a sharp eye on everything that passed, from brooks and children up, and that if she noticed anything odd or out of place she would never rest until she had ferreted *out the whys and wherefores thereof.*

Can you guess the meaning of ferreted?
Read the sentence again- *she would never rest until she had* _____ *out the whys and wherefores thereof.*

Guess the meaning - Reading augments vocabulary. Using context clues to understand the meaning of a word is a great way to enhance vocabulary. It is sometimes easier to figure out the meaning of the word by the way it is used in a sentence.

WEEK 6

This week, you will be learning CHALLENGING WORDS.

Remember - Reading augments vocabulary.

Have you ever guessed the meaning of a word that you don't know?

Yes! Whenever I read a book. I do that quite often but I also make sure to check its meaning afterward.

▶ **Activity 10** Read the sentences given below and try to guess the meaning of the word. Use a dictionary to check if you guessed correctly.

1. Intrepid
adjective

The intrepid explorer set out on the dangerous voyage.

I **think** it means…

It **actually** means…

----

2. Frugal
adjective

My uncle is frugal and spends money very wisely.

I **think** it means…

It **actually** means…

----

3. Nefarious
adjective

People kept walking in and out of doors with nefarious purpose.

I **think** it means…

It **actually** means…

4. Truncate
verb

Leah is going to truncate the time she spends at work.

I **think** it means...

It **actually** means...

----

5. Procrastinate
verb

Sam procrastinated until the last minute and had to stay up all night to finish his work.

I **think** it means...

It **actually** means...

----

6. Mendacious
adjective

Leah was being mendacious about what really happened at school.

I **think** it means...

It **actually** means...

7. Hapless
adjective

Harry considered himself as the most hapless person due to a series of unfortunate events.

I **think** it means...

It actually means...

----

8. Indolent
adjective

Despite his being so knowledgeable, Sam's indolent attitude meant he could never finish his assignments on time.

I **think** it means...

It **actually** means...

----

9. Entrancing
adjective

The short story written by Zoe was entrancing and thrilling for the reader.

I **think** it means...

It **actually** means...

10. Deleterious
adjective

Excessive use of drugs can have a deleterious effect on the nervous system.

I **think** it means...

It actually means...

----

11. Garrulous
adjective

She talked too much about herself like a garrulous fool.

I **think** it means...

It **actually** means...

----

12. Sagacious
adjective

The sagacious inventor went from rags to riches with one great idea.

I **think** it means...

It **actually** means...

41

You have learnt so far

(Part of speech) (Root words) (Prefixes and suffixes) (Synonyms and Antonyms)
(Homophones) (Adverbs) (Challenging words)

Practice task 5 – Week 6

This week your task is to collect all the new words ⭐ you have encountered while reading a book. Write down the title of the book and the page number you have taken the words from.

At the end of the day, re-read each sentence in which an unfamiliar word appears, and using your perception, write down what you think is the meaning of the word. Lastly, consult the dictionary to check the meaning and see if you have guessed correctly. Practice this activity for a week. This will increase your comprehension skills.

Word	I think it means...	I know it means...

Replacing overused words

Making a list of overused words and replacing them with more sophisticated ones helps widen vocabulary and improves writing skills. This activity will help you to engage consciously with new words. The understanding of a new word or knowledge builds in three layers; *we start with what we know, we add new information in relation to what we know and we expand word knowledge.*

Moreover, replacing the repetitive words with more interesting vocabulary adds depth to writing. The skilled use of a wide array of words enables you to portray your imagination vividly and assists you to express ideas astutely. Knowing the synonyms of commonly used words is an easy way to boost vocabulary.

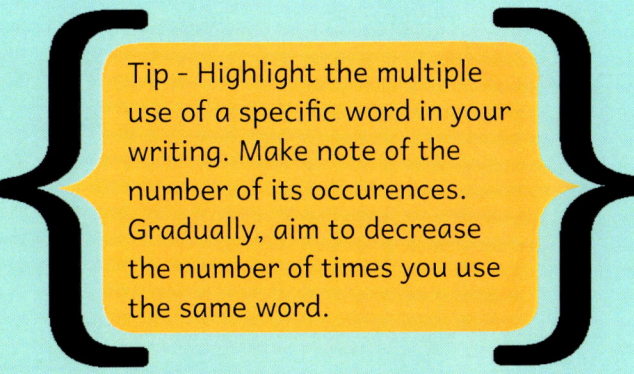

Tip - Highlight the multiple use of a specific word in your writing. Make note of the number of its occurences. Gradually, aim to decrease the number of times you use the same word.

then - later on, eventually, afterwards, finally

but - however, nevertheless, nonetheless

so - therefore, consequently, hence

Replacing overused words - Making a list of overused words and replacing it with more sophisticated ones can help you enhance your vocabulary and improves writing skills.

WEEK 7

This week, you will be learning OVERUSED WORDS.

Remember - A wide array of words enhances the ability to express ideas.

The repetition of the same words over and over again makes writing boring; while the skilled use of a wide array of words enables you to portray your imagination vividly and assists you to express your ideas astutely. It is vital to know the synonyms to replace the commonly used words.

The weather is very warm. It's making me very happy. I am very hungry.

That sounds so boring. Can you think of words to replace very?

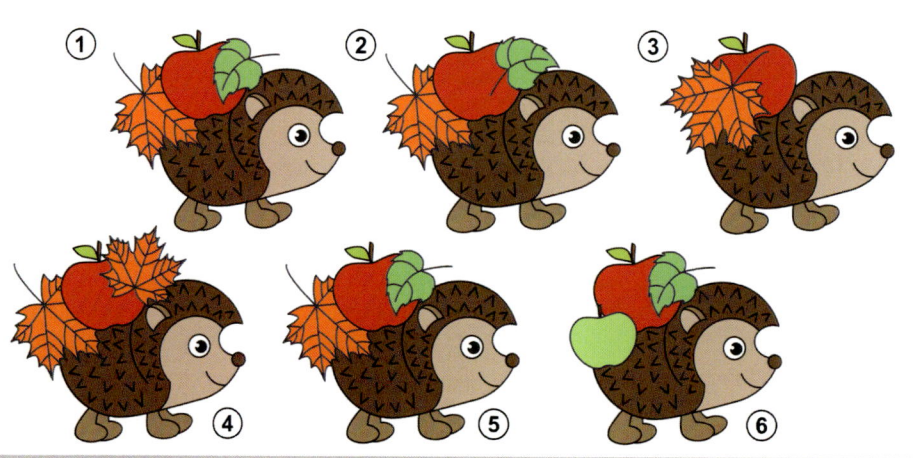

Fab V OCAB

➤ **Activity 11**   Write as many synonyms as you can for the word given below.

Happy - How to say you are happy without using the word happy?

	Word	Meaning
1.	**Glad** (adj.)	Happy and pleased about something.
2.		
3.		
4.		
5.		
6.		
7.		
8.		
9.		
10.		
11.		
12.		
13.		
14.		
15.		
16.		
17.		
18.		
19.		

Fab V OCAB

	Word	Meaning
1.	**Unhappy** (adj.)	Feeling sad or upset
2.		
3.		
4.		
5.		
6.		
7.		
8.		
9.		
10.		
11.		
12.		
13.		
14.		
15.		
16.		
17.		
18.		
19.		

20.	
21.	
22.	
23.	
24.	

Angry – How to say you are angry without using the word angry?

	Word	Meaning
1.	**Annoyed** (adj.)	feeling slightly angry or impatient.
2.		
3.		
4.		
5.		
6.		
7.		
8.		
9.		
10.		
11.		
12.		
13.		

FabOCAB

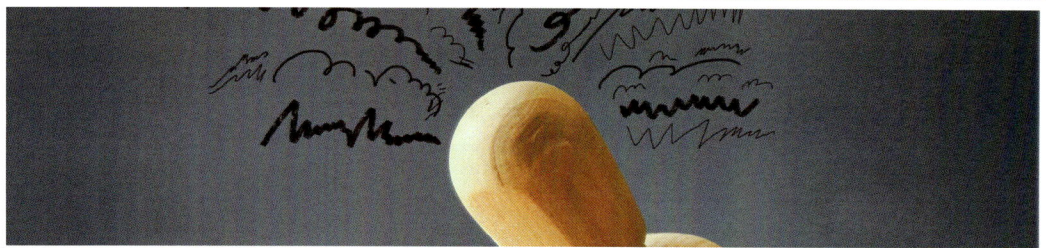

	Word	Meaning
1.	Frightened (adj.)	very nervous or worried.
2.		
3.		
4.		
5.		
6.		
7.		
8.		
9.		
10.		
11.		
12.		
13.		
14.		
15.		
16.		
17.		
18.		

Find three synonyms of the adjectives given below.

1. Brave			
2. Evil			
3. Curious			
4. Lazy			
. Cheerful			
. Glum			
. Kind			

8.   Selfish

9.   Intelligent

10.   Funny

Find three synonyms of the verbs given below.

11.   Start

12.   Continue

13.   Laugh

14.   Decrease

15.   Look

16.   Fulfil

17.   Ignite

18.   Lurk

19.   Fall

20.   Walk

 Find three synonyms of the words given below.

21.   Hungry

22.   Hide

23.   Run

24. Keep			
25. Difference			
26. Help			
27. Understand			
28. Show			
29. Get			
30. Strange			

You have learnt so far

(Part of speech) (Root words) (Prefixes and suffixes) (Synonyms and Antonyms) (Homophones) (Adverbs) (Overused words)

Practice task 06 – Week 7 The task for this week is to make a list of words that you use quite often in your writing or conversation. Use a thesaurus to find out at least three synonyms of these words. Encourage yourself to replace the words that you frequently use with their synonyms.

Word	Synonyms

Activity-1
(Noun to verb)
1. procrastination - procrastinate
2. beautician- beautify
3. completion - complete
4. enhancement - enhance
5. embarkment - embark
6. persuasion - persuade

Activity - 2
(Adjective to adverb)
1. fabulous - fabulously
2. diligent - diligently
3. benevolent - benevolently
4. astute - astutely
5. avid - avidly
6. meek - meekly

Activity -3
Nouns - ocean, country, statue of liberty, milk, happiness, audience
Pronouns - they, everybody, none, several, myself, whoever
Adjectives - shaggy, spectacular, coarse, breezy, cantankerous, copious
Verbs - should, clean, seem, been, sprint, gaze
Adverbs - extremely, whenever, adoringly, savagely, annually, tomorrow, regardless
Prepositions - under, across, despite, before, without
Conjunctions - although, since, yet, whenever, after, but, regarding
Interjections - cheers, congratulations, phew, ouch, hello, thanks

Activity- 4
Meaning of the word 'VARI' is different, change. The origin is Latin.
1. **Variation** - Change or slight difference
2. **Variety** - state of being different
3. **Invariable** - never changing
4. **Varied** - several different types
5. **Variance** - the quality of being different
6. **Covariant** - varying with something else to preserve certain mathematical interrelations

Activity-5
1. **Bio - life, origin (Greek). Biology**- study of living things. **Biography**- an account of someone's life. **Biodegradable**- capable of being decomposed by bacteria or other living organisms. 2. **Pater -father, origin (Latin). Paternal**- related to father. **Patriarch** – male head of a family or tribe. **Paternity** – the fact or stage of being a father.
3. **Sign – mark , origin (Latin). Design** - drawing. **Signal**- a gesture, action or sound to give a particular message. **Signature**- a distinctive mark.
4. **Spect - see, origin (Latin). Introspect** -to examine your own ideas, thoughts, and feelings, **Spectacle**- a public event or show that is exciting to watch, Glasses . **Spectre**- a mental image of something unpleasant
5. **Gen - birth, origin (Greek). Generate**- to cause something to exist. **Progeny** - offspring. **Genesis**- formation
6. **Chrono – time, origin (Greek). Chronological**- the order in which a series of events happened. **Chronical**- relating to or controlled by time. **Synchronise**- occur at the same time or rate

Activity-6

(Word)	(prefix)	(New word)	(Meaning)
1. correct	in	incorrect	not correct
2. approve	dis	disapprove	to refuse to approve
3. behave	mis	misbehave	to behave wrongly
4. tell	re	retell	to tell something again
5. conventional	un	unconventional	not following accepted practices or rules

(Word)	(suffix)	(New word)	(Meaning)
1. heart	less	heartless	merciless
2. beauty	ful	beautiful	full of beauty
3. love	able	loveable	deserving love
4. affectionate	ly	affectionately	lovingly
5. smart	est	smartest	the most intelligent

Activity 7 - Synonyms and Antonyms (Echo Valley)

1. **Amenable - If you are amenable to something, you are willing to do it or accept it.**
   a.   **Synonym -** receptive, responsive, open
   b.   **Antonym -** uncooperative, resistant, unamenable

2. **Dismal - something which is bad in a sad or depressing way.**
   a.   **Synonym -** dreary, mournful, doleful
   b.   **Antonym -** bright, cheerful, vibrant

3. **Proficient - If you are proficient in something, you can do it well.**
   a.   **Synonym -** skilled, adept, expert
   b.   **Antonym -** incompetent, inept, incapable

4. **Taciturn – A taciturn person does not say very much and can seem unfriendly.**
   a.   **Synonym -** reticent, quiet, reserved
   b.   **Antonym -** loquacious, talkative, garrulous

5. **Audacious - Someone who is audacious takes risks in order to achieve something**
   a.   **Synonym -** daring, bold, enterprising
   b.   **Antonym -** timid, cowardly, cautious

6. **Obstinate - you describe someone as obstinate; you are being critical of them because they are very determined to do what they want, and refuse to change their mind.**
   a.   **Synonym -** stubborn, determined, persistent
   b.   **Antonym -** amenable, aggregable, compliant

7. **Exuberant adj. - If you are exuberant, you are full of energy, excitement, and cheerfulness.**
   a.   **Synonym -** energetic, enthusiastic, animated
   b.   **Antonym -** dull, lifeless, subdued

8. **Oblivious - If you are oblivious to something or oblivious of it, you are not aware of it.**
   a. **Synonym -** ignorant, unaware, negligent
   b. **Antonym -** alert, observant, attentive

9. **Riveting - extremely interesting and exciting**
   a. **Synonym -** enthralling, fascinating, captivating
   b. **Antonym -** boring, dull, monotonous

10. **Exquisite - something that is exquisite is extremely beautiful or pleasant**
    a. **Synonym -** elegant, beautiful, graceful
    b. **Antonym -** ugly, unattractive, unlovely

11. **Petrified - if you are petrified, you are extremely frightened**
    a. **Synonym -** terrified, horrified, stunned
    b. **Antonym -** composed, dauntless, audacious

12. **Exasperated - frustrated or angry**
    a. **Synonym -** infuriated, enraged, incensed
    b. **Antonym -** content, cheerful, calm

13. **Apprehensive - Someone who is apprehensive is afraid that something bad may happen.**
    a. **Synonym -** anxious, nervous, concerned
    b. **Antonym -** confident, assured, composed

14. **Destitute - Someone who is destitute has no money or possessions.**
    a. **Synonym -** penniless, poor, impoverished
    b. **Antonym -** rich, affluent, wealthy

15. **Savage - Someone or something that is savage is extremely cruel**
    a. **Synonym -** brutal, vicious, fierce
    b. **Antonym -** humane, kind, gentle

Activity 8 - Homophones - Page 20

1. **discreet (adjective)** - careful and prudent in one's speech or actions, especially in order to keep something confidential. / **discrete (adjective)** - individually separate and distinct.
2. **eminent (adjective)** – high in station, rank, or repute / **imminent (adjective)** - about to happen.
3. **extant (adjective)** - still in existence; surviving. / **extent (noun)** - the area covered by something.
4. **precede (verb)**– come before (something) in time. / **proceed (verb)** - begin a course of action.
5. **insight(noun) -** the capacity to gain an accurate and deep understanding of someone or something.
   incite (verb) - encourage or stir up (violent or unlawful behaviour.
6. **principal (noun)** - head of school.
   principle(noun)- a fundamental truth or proposition that serves as the foundation for a system of belief.
7. **peal (noun)** – a loud ringing of a bell or bells. / **peel (noun)**- skin of a fruit.
8. **currant (noun)** - a small dried fruit made from a small seedless variety of grape.
   current (adjective) - belonging to the present time.

9. **descent (noun)** - an act of moving downwards.

   dissent (noun)- the holding or expression of opinions at variance with those commonly or officially held.

10. **bough (noun)** – a main branch of a tree. / **bow (noun)**- a knot tied with two loops and two loose ends.

11. **waive (verb)** - Refrain from insisting on or using (a right or claim). / **wave (noun)** - a raised line of water that moves across the surface of an area of water, especially the sea.

12. **quire (noun)** - four sheets of paper or parchment folded to form eight leaves / **choir (noun)**- an organized group of singers.

13. **hoard (noun)** - a stock or store of money or valued objects. / **horde (noun)**- a large group of people.

14. **vain (adjective)** - useless/ **vein (noun)**- blood vessels.

Activity 9 - Adverbs

1. **Bashfully –** in a nervous or timid manner
2. **Sheepishly –** in a way that is embarrassed because you have done something wrong or silly
3. **Hysterically –** in an uncontrolled way, because you are extremely frightened, angry, excited
4. **Woefully –** in a very sad way to emphasise how bad a situation is
5. **Valiantly –** in a way that is very brave or determined
6. **Obnoxiously –** in an extremely unpleasant way
7. **Affectionately –** in a way that shows liking or love
8. **Strenuously –** in a way that needs or uses great effort and energy
9. **Avidly –** in an extremely eager or interested way
10. **Briskly –** in a quick and energetic way
11. **Vivaciously –** in a way that is attractively energetic and enthusiastic
12. **Coaxingly –** in a way that persuades someone gently to do something, by being kind or patient, or by appearing to be
13. **Elegantly –** in a way that is graceful and attractive in appearance or behaviour
14. **Outrageously –** in a very shocking or unacceptable way
15. **Queasily –** in a way that makes you feel worried, unhappy, or uncertain

Activity 10- Challenging words

1. **Intrepid – fearless, bold**

   Synonyms: courageous, audacious. **Antonyms:** fearful, cowardly, measly / The **intrepid** explorer set out on the dangerous voyage.

2. **Frugal – economical in use or expenditure**

   Synonyms: thrifty, prudent. **Antonyms:** extravagant, lavish / My uncle is **frugal** and spends money very wisely.

3. **Nefarious – evil**

   Synonyms: wicked, sinful. **Antonyms:** ethical, righteous

   People kept walking in and out of doors with **nefarious** purpose.

4.   Truncate – cut short

Synonyms: short, trim, curtail. **Antonyms:** enlarge, expand, elongate / Ria is going to **truncate** the time she spends at work.

5.   Procrastinate – delay

Synonyms – postpone, adjourn, drag out. **Antonyms:** accelerate, quicken, go ahead
Sam **procrastinated** until the last minute and had to stay up all night to finish his work.

6.   Mendacious – untruthful

Synonyms: lying, deceitful, dishonest. **Antonyms:** honest, truthful
Leah was being **mendacious** about what really happened at school.

7.   Hapless – unlucky

Synonyms: ill-fated, unfortunate, pitiful. **Antonyms:** lucky, fortunate
Harry considered himself as the most **hapless** person due to a series of unfortunate events.

8.   Indolent – lazy

Synonyms: lethargic, torpid, idle. **Antonyms:** industrious, diligent
Despite his being so knowledgeable, Sam's **indolent** attitude meant he could never finish his assignments on time.

9.   Entrancing – to fill with delight or wonder

Synonyms: enticing, fascinating. **Antonyms:** boring, dull
The short story written by Zoe was **entrancing** and thrilling for the reader.

10.   Deleterious – harmful

Synonyms: damaging, detrimental. **Antonyms:** harmless, innocuous
Excessive use of drugs can have a **deleterious** effect on the nervous system.

11.   Garrulous – chatty

Synonyms: chatty, talkative. **Antonyms:** taciturn, untalkative
She talked too much about herself like a **garrulous** fool.

12.   Sagacious – wise

Synonyms-canny, astute. **Antonyms:** unintelligent, foolish
The **sagacious** inventor went from rags to riches with one great idea.

Activity 11 – Happy

1. **Glad** (adj.) – happy and pleased about something.
2. **Pleased** (adj.) – happy and satisfied.
3. **Content** (adj.) – happy and satisfied with your life.
4. **Cheerful** (adj.) – behaving in a happy friendly way.
5. **Exuberant** (adj.) – happy, excited, and full of energy.
6. **Buoyant** (adj.) – feeling happy and confident.
7. **Chirpy** (adj.) – happy and lively.
8. **Chuffed** (adj.) – extremely happy.
9. **Delighted** (adj.) – very happy, especially because something good has happened.
10. **Delirious** (adj.) – extremely happy and excited.
11. **Ebullient** (adj.) – very happy and enthusiastic.
12. **Ecstatic** (adj.) – extremely happy or pleased.
13. **Elated** (adj.) – extremely happy and excited.
14. **Euphoric** (adj.) – feeling extremely happy, usually for a short time only.
15. **Exalted** (adj.) – extremely happy and proud.
16. **Exhilarated** (adj.) – extremely happy, excited, and full of energy.
17. **Gleeful** (adj.) – happy and excited, often because of someone else's bad luck.
18. **Joyful** (adj.) – very happy.
19. **Jubilant** (adj.) – extremely happy because something good has happened.

Activity 11 – Sad

1. **Unhappy** (adj.) – feeling sad or upset.
2. **Sombre** (adj.) – serious, or sad.
3. **Melancholy** (adj.) – feeling or looking sad and without hope, or making you feel sad and without hope.
4. **Sorrowful** (adj.) – feeling, expressing, or causing great sadness.
5. **Bleak** (adj.) – without any reasons to feel happy or hopeful.
6. **Wistful** (adj.) – slightly sad because you want to have or to do something.
7. **Depressed** (adj.) – if you are depressed, you feel very unhappy because of a difficult or unpleasant situation that you feel you cannot change.
8. **Desolate** (adj.) – feeling very sad and lonely.
9. **Despondent** (adj.) – very unhappy because you do not believe that an unpleasant situation will improve.
10. **Devastated** (adj.) – severe and overwhelming shock or grief.
11. **Disconsolate** (adj.) – extremely unhappy or disappointed.
12. **Distressed** (adj.) – very unhappy, worried, or upset.
13. **Forlorn** (adj.) – appearing lonely and sad.
14. **Gloomy** (adj.) – showing that things are not going well and will probably not go well in the future.
15. **Glum** (adj.) – looking sad, as if you expect something bad to happen
16. **Grumpy** (adj.) – unhappy and dissatisfied, often for no obvious reason.
17. **Miserable** (adj.) – extremely unhappy or uncomfortable.
18. **Morose** (adj.) – feeling unhappy, in a bad mood, and not wanting to talk to anyone.
19. **Mournful** (adj.) – very sad.
20. **Shattered** (adj.) – extremely upset.
21. **Upset** (adj.) – very sad, worried, or angry about something.
22. **Woeful** (adj.) – feeling very sad.
23. **Wretched** (adj.) – very unhappy, or ill.

Activity 11 - Angry

1. **Annoyed** (adj.) - feeling slightly angry or impatient.
2. **Upset** (adj.) - very sad, worried, or angry about something.
3. **Displeased** (adj.) - formal annoyed or angry, usually because something is not very good or someone has made a mistake.
4. **Bitter** (adj.) - feeling angry or upset because of a bad experience, especially when you think that you have been treated unfairly.
5. **Disgusted** (adj.) - feeling very angry and upset about something that you do not approve of.
6. **Embittered** (adj.) - angry and unhappy about things that have happened to you in the past.
7. **Exasperated** (adj.) - extremely annoyed and impatient because things are not happening in the way that you want or people are not doing what you want them to do.
8. **Frustrated** (adj.) - feeling annoyed and impatient because you are prevented from achieving something.
9. **Grim** (adj.) - angry and pleased about something at the same time.
10. **Piqued** (adj.)- slightly annoyed and offended.
11. **Resentful** (adj.) - feeling angry and unhappy because you think you have been treated unfairly or without enough respect.
12. **Irate** (adj.) - very angry.
13. **Sulky** (adj.) - feeling angry and unhappy and not wanting to talk to anyone or to be with other people.

Activity 11 - Worried

1. **Frightened** (adj.) - very nervous or worried.
2. **Troubled** (adj.) - worried about the problems that you have.
3. **Agitated** (adj.) - worried or upset.
4. **Alarmed** (adj.) - frightened or worried that something unpleasant or dangerous might happen.
5. **Apprehensive** (adj.) - slightly worried or nervous.
6. **Concerned** (adj.) - worried about something.
7. **Distraught** (adj.) - extremely worried, upset, or confused.
8. **Frantic** (adj.) - so worried or upset that you are not able to control your feelings.
9. **Fraught** (adj.) - very worried and with a lot of problems.
10. **Fretful** (adj.) - worried and unhappy, especially because of being nervous or tired.
11. **Neurotic** (adj.) - extremely worried about something unimportant in a way that does not seem reasonable to other people.
12. **Panic** (adj.) - feeling so afraid or worried that you cannot think clearly or calmly.
13. **Paranoid** (adj.) - worrying that people do not like you and are trying to harm you, although you have no proof of this.
14. **Perturbed** (adj.) - worried or upset by something.
15. **Scared** (adj.) - appearing worried or upset.
16. **Shaken** (adj.) - feeling nervous or frightened because of something that has happened.
17. **Vexed** (adj.) - annoyed, confused, or worried.

Find three synonyms of the adjectives given below.

1. **Brave** – gallant, courageous, valiant
2. **Evil** – hideous, grisly, sinful
3. **Curious** – inquiring, analytical, eager
4. **Lazy** – indolent, inactive, inert
5. **Cheerful** – animated, jaunty, perky
6. **Glum** – mournful, despondent, dejected
7. **Kind** – compassionate, amiable, generous
8. **Selfish** – greedy, envious, avaricious
9. **Intelligent** – ingenious, wise, astute
10. **Funny** – comical, amusing, jovial

11. **Start** – commence, begin, initiate
12. **Continue** – pursue, perpetuate, persevere
13. **Laugh** – chuckle, giggle, cackle
14. **Accomplish** – fulfil, complete, achieve
15. **Ignite** – incinerate, kindle, light
16. **Lurk** – prowl, sneak, slink
17. **Fall** – tumble, topple, plunge
18. **Walk** – stroll, saunter, amble
19. **Decrease** – diminish, wither, wane
20. **Look** – gaze, glance, gape

21. **Hungry** – ravenous, starving, famished
22. **Hide** – conceal, mask, shroud
23. **Run** – dash, sprint, scamper
24. **Keep** – hold, retain, preserve
25. **Difference** – inequality, dissimilarity, disparity
26. **Help** – assist, aid, support
27. **Understand** – discern, comprehend, perceive
28. **Show** – display, exhibit, reveal
29. **Get** – acquire, obtain, secure
30. **Strange** – bizarre, peculiar, queer

Ideal to buy with this book -

Our vocabulary flash cards pack is ideal for learning new words with ease. The pack contains word cards with parts of speech, synonyms, antonyms and a sample sentence, homophones, root words, commonly used words, overused words. Ideal for 11 PLUS preparation, these cards are colour coded to facilitate learning.

Please email us at **info@authorinme.com** for any query regarding the cards.

Vocabulary Cards for Ks2 and 11 PLUS

Excellent revision tool
Engaging classroom activity
Makes vocabulary learning manageable
Colour coded for easy learning
Available on Amazon and bookstores

"Splended collection of words."
    - Alice Hemming, author

"A concise list of relevant words."
    - Karen Smith, parent

"A vital tool to make word learning fun."
    - Sherry Narula, English teacher